T0195558

MAN OF GOD: WHAT IS YOUR REPORT?

Written By
Anointed Men of God

**Corey Ellis, I ~ Bobby Lowe
Raymonda Speller ~ Marco Mays
Bennie Liggins ~ Anthony Brock ~ Keith Moore
Thomas Tucker, IV ~ Anderson Graves, II
Carl Shamburger, Jr. ~ Warrick Maye
JR Gaines ~ Tosh Sevier, I**

Compiled & Edited By

W. R. Coleman

authorHOUSE

AuthorHouse™
1663 Liberty Drive
Bloomington, IN 47403
www.authorhouse.com
Phone: 1 (800) 839-8640

Published by AuthorHouse 02/17/2020

ISBN: 978-1-7283-4735-6 (sc)
ISBN: 978-1-7283-4734-9 (e)

Library of Congress Control Number: 2020903098

Print information available on the last page.

Any people depicted in stock imagery provided by Getty Images are models, and such images are being used for illustrative purposes only. Certain stock imagery © Getty Images.

Unless otherwise indicated, all scripture quotations are from The Holy Bible, English Standard Version® (ESV®). Copyright ©2001 by Crossway Bibles, a division of Good News Publishers. Used by permission. All rights reserved.

Scripture quotations marked NIV are taken from the Holy Bible, New International Version®. NIV®. Copyright © 1973, 1978, 1984 by International Bible Society. Used by permission of Zondervan. All rights reserved. [Biblica]

Scripture quotations marked NKJV are taken from the New King James Version. Copyright © 1982 by Thomas Nelson, Inc. Used by permission. All rights reserved.

Scripture quotations marked KJV are from the Holy Bible, King James Version (Authorized Version). First published in 1611. Quoted from the KJV Classic Reference Bible, Copyright © 1983 by The Zondervan Corporation.

This book is printed on acid-free paper.

Dedicated to the Man of God
who taught me & my four sisters
how to stand up for God,
pray without ceasing, and
work to give Him Glory.

Thank You, Mr. Joseph L. Coleman,
for being Our Example, Our Pattern, Our Provider
Our Daddy.

Foreword

The faithfulness of God has always amazed me. Even when I was a child, there was something that drew me into the Word of God, a hunger that has only grown and increased over the years. My passion for writing is a manifestation of that amazement and hunger, and now that God has opened the doors through which this passion can truly live – I am even more amazed! This second book in THE REPORT SERIES is more than encouragement for me. It is yet another proof of God's faithfulness to me.

I heard the title for this series over 15 years ago, but at that time, I was struggling to believe that writing, publishing, and creating opportunities for others to express themselves in print could ever *really* be something I could accomplish. But God . . . in the fullness of time and in the right season, He allowed me to publish my first book in 2011. Now we're on number three with several other projects already planned. I tell you that GOD IS FAITHFUL!

The Anointed Men of God in this volume come from all walks of life: entrepreneurs, judges, educators, pastors, trainers. You name it, and they are probably within these pages. Each of them readily accepted the invitation to share their "reports" and when you read them, I declare you'll be blessed! Some shared that they've always had a desire to be published. Some said they always wanted to tell their story. Some even asked, "You sure you want *me* to write something?" My response to all of these was the same: GOD IS FAITHFUL!

Thank You for making the investment and taking the time to experience *Man of God: What Is Your Report?* I have no doubt you will be inspired, blessed, challenged, intrigued, and waiting on the next volume with much anticipation.

Blessings & Life to You,
W. R. Coleman

Get Your MIND Right: Your Body Will Follow!

COREY ELLIS, I

A little over 14 years ago, my family and I were evacuating from what is now known as one of the most devastating natural disasters in U.S. history: Hurricane Katrina. Sometimes I reminisce on the good times my friends and I shared in New Orleans as well as all we possessed that was destroyed, washed away, and left behind. I allow my mind back only briefly because I have learned how powerful the mind is. From those moments of somewhat painful memories, I quickly refocus on what God has allowed me to gain since then: two amazing children, success in the personal training arena, entrepreneurship, and connections with some great people in the Montgomery community. If I had tried to script the way my life would pan out after Katrina, I would not have scraped the surface of fathoming the blessings that have been granted and received. But this one thing I do know: the greatest battles and the strongest triumphs have manifested when I forced my MIND to line up with my SPIRIT . . . and my physical man had to follow.

This is the mindset with which I approach my professional connection with my clients. I am so grateful that over the past 14 years since I began my fitness career, it has worked time and time again. The results that God and hard work have allowed my clients to realize are nothing short of amazing. But the results don't

1

come for RezFIT family members (or anyone else for that matter) without achieving the MINDSET that enables success. It is a mindset that says, "My body might not want to do the work and my spirit is having its own battles, but I've got a **mind** to do it!"

> *Well after years of hearing Corey tell me not to quit and keep pushing, it has become my mindset. When I want to quit, I can hear him say, "You quit and ten more!"*
> RezFIT Client Testimony

I try to get the most from my clients. My method of training and of living incorporates care and concern that might not look like it all the time. I aspire to help each and every individual achieve the health and wellness goal, he or she has set for themselves. They say I'm tough, but if the process was easy, everyone would do it with readiness – and I'd be useless. The journey to personal fitness is difficult no lie. It's filled will a lot of "I can't" or "what I use to could do." Many times, the road to better health through exercise is paved with "this isn't working, so why keep doing it?" We must have a tenacious, focused, won't quit motivating mechanism to undertake a difficult journey like this. That's why I press forward with the mission, and my method to getting my clients to their goals. It works. It gets RESULTS.

> *Just trust the process. It's a love-hate relationship and always is when trying to get the results you want. One day you will look back and just be so thankful for all those days you wanted to strangle your trainer. It's a life change if you choose it. I am so glad for the day I signed up!*
> RezFIT Client Testimony

Your body will go to the next level, if your mind leads it. The journey is real and tough because it's constant. It's every day, every hour, every minute. Within that just strive to do better each day, hour, minute. It is in the striving, the trying, the relentless determination to reach another level that the results show up in fitness – AND IN LIFE. The parallel is undeniable. The same measure of commitment that I try to inspire in my clients is also what it takes to keep us committed in life. Whether it is to your family, your career, your relationship with God, or getting up to walk the dog every morning: it all takes a committed mind that will connect with a strong spirit. AND GETTING THE MIND RIGHT DOES A BODY GOOD.

Sometimes goals and visions get lost or become hazy on the way to achieving them. This can be especially true when it seems you are the only one who values your goals and believes in your visions. But that's okay because that is the beauty in setting goals and pursuing visions. Visions are not meant for EVERYONE to see. Nor do we have to take the same path towards success. The battle is to keep the goals and visions in the forefront. Whatever it is and wherever that may be: IT IS YOURS. EMBRACE. PROTECT. IMPLEMENT. Moving towards higher heights requires that you open your eyes and become aware of every SINGLE thing. And let your MIND understand this truth - if you don't want to go through trials, don't aspire to be great.

> *And three years later, I ran in and*
> *completed my first half marathon!*
> *Corey's training stays with you even if you*
> *fall off . . . You can pick it up again.*
> *He's going to be right there yelling at you: Keep trying!*
> RezFIT Client Testimony

I am often asked "how do I stay motivated over time?" Staying motivated to maintain a healthy lifestyle of eating and exercise takes a consistent and POSITIVE MINDSET. We must try to keep negative phrases out of our vocabulary. "I can't, I don't think I can, and I feel like a failure" are all fuel that ignites a fire of self-defeat every time. Striving to live a healthier lifestyle is definitely one of the most difficult things some individuals will undertake. This doesn't make them bad people. It doesn't mean that they're lazy. It doesn't mean that they are anything less than others. Motivation requires us to understand this.

It also requires an atmosphere filled with positive people with the same positive mindset. That mindset is one of striving for some of the same goals including living healthier. Some people around us will have to be removed from our immediate circle for a while just so we can gain control over our mind and actions towards exercise, food, training, etc. Nevertheless, IT IS ALREADY WITHIN YOU. It is a personal decision to take full control of your MINDSET and be able to fulfill the fitness goals, good health, the physique that you choose to obtain for yourself! It is all in the MINDSET!

> *I don't need a scale to tell me about the change Corey Ellis and a healthier lifestyle have made in me. All I have to do is look at a few pictures of the 'old' me! I think back on the times when I was sad and trapped in a body that I didn't care for at all, living half my life! But NO MORE! Let's take control of our minds and treat our bodies like the temples they are!*
> RezFIT Client Testimony

Are you on the road to your mission in life? Are you striving towards a purpose and goal for self? If you are an individual that presses toward progression daily, like I strive to be, NEVER allow anyone to place his or her LIMITED IMAGINATION on you and hinder you from the success that lives within you. Sometimes others have such shallow minds when they formulate their perception of you. But when it comes to God's plan and purpose for your life, NEVER let anyone put you in a box where you don't belong. Keep pushing toward your dreams and aspirations, and never fall into the trap of someone else's LIMITED IMAGINATION of you. To be in tune with oneself - MIND, SPIRIT, AND BODY - is a powerful attribute to possess.

Here's my closing word of encouragement to you: Love yourself. Be yourself. Do you! Who cares if people talk about you or what they say about you? If you're doing well or if you're down in the dumps, people are going to talk (good or bad). Continue to do you! Those situations, obstacles, or circumstances you cannot control, let them be. Your character is built on how you handle it (right or wrong). Stay focused. Never worry. KEEP YOUR MIND RIGHT.

If you've never seen anyone get a fresh start to re-live his or her life in a different way, you have now by way of this report! Through a horrendously devastating natural disaster man named Katrina, I truly got that opportunity at 23 years old. I haven't looked back since. I thank all the citizens of Montgomery for the continual support over the years. There's more work for me to do, and I am ready to do it! Man named her Katrina. I refer to her as OPPORTUNITY.

Corey Ellis, I is renown in the River Region as the consummate personal trainer and fitness specialist. His growing entrepreneurial presence is centered around RESOLUTION FITNESS (RezFIT at 3440 Atlanta Highway in Montgomery) and impacts hundreds of clients weekly through his 5-Week Boot Camp Challenges, personal training, and even partnership with Planet Fitness on Atlanta Highway in Montgomery. Corey's greatest accomplishments, however, are his two amazing, talented, and brilliant children Lourdes & Corey II,  affectionately known as Dos. Along with his supportive mother, Cathy Ellis-Jones, Corey strives to fulfill RezFIT's primary mission of "Helping People Help Themselves."

In Sickness and In Health: When Unconditional Love Matters

DR. BOBBY L. LOWE

Introduction

On April 7, 2019, Dr. Wendy R. Coleman, my beloved pastor of Reaching the Remnant Ministries, asked me if I would be a contributor to her upcoming book, titled "Man of God: What is Your Report?" Without hesitation, I quickly said yes - even without knowing all the details. However, quickly saying yes did not surprise me. I have always been proactive and a person who did not fear the unknown. Deuteronomy 31:6 (NKJV) states, *"Be strong and of good courage, do not fear nor be afraid of them; for the LORD your God, He is the One who goes with you. He will not leave you nor forsake you."* A few hours later, Pastor Coleman emailed me, revealing the details and proposing my topic: "In Sickness and In Health: When Unconditional Love Matters."

What Is Unconditional Love?

In thought, I asked myself: What exactly is unconditional love? I know you cannot go to your local supermarket and grab a can of unconditional love off the shelf and proceed to the checkout counter. Nor can you knock on your neighbor's door and ask to borrow a cup of unconditional love. That's because unconditional love is abstract, meaning "it is the existing in thought or as an idea but not having a physical or concrete existence" (English Oxford Dictionary).

1 Corinthians 13:4-7 (ESV) states, "*Love is patient and kind; love does not envy or boast; it is not arrogant or rude. It does not insist on its own way; it is not irritable or resentful; it does not rejoice at wrongdoing but rejoices with the truth. Love bears all things, believes all things, hopes all things, endures all things.*" Consequently, I have concluded it would be best to give my report by describing and demonstrating my unconditional love for my wife, especially when it mattered - in sickness and in health, as God requested. John 15:12 (ESV) states, "*This is my commandment, that you love one another as I have loved you.*"

My Report

A Product of Your Environment

I grew up as the third oldest of six siblings in a small, peaceful, rural town in northeast Mississippi where everyone was friendly and considered family. My mother and father were great parents who exhibited great love for each other and their children their entire lives. My father was a tall, muscular man. My mother was a short, petite woman. My father was the "bread winner" of the family and taught me how to maintain a home and protect and provide for others. In fact, I probably could operate any machinery, drive any automobile, and plant and grow any vegetable by age 12.

My mother also taught me lifelong skills, such as how to cook, housekeep, do laundry, press clothes, decorate, and pot and grow flowers. But most importantly, they were loving and God-fearing parents, and ones that should be emulated. They also made sure we knew and served God and did His work within the community. In fact, I recall one Sunday morning when my parents grabbed all six of us and proceeded to church to be baptized. At the time, some of us probably did not know the true meaning of baptism, but there was one thing I did know. I felt like I was on the right pathway for bigger and brighter things because I had accepted God in my life. In Acts 2:38-39 (ESV), *"**And Peter said to them, 'Repent and be baptized every one of you in the name of Jesus Christ for the forgiveness of your sins, and you will receive the gift of the Holy Spirit. The promise is for you and your children and for all who are far off—for all whom the Lord our God will call.'"**

A Childhood Girlfriend

Like many young boys who were star athletes in high school, I had fun playing sports and only did well enough in school just to continue to play sports. I knew I was much smarter than this, but at the time, I really did not care. However, I always questioned this behavior because deep within my heart I knew this was wrong. Therefore, I decided to stop this behavior and to start focusing more on God and graduating from high school during my senior year. *"**When I was a child, talked like a child, I thought like a child, I reasoned like a child. When I became a man, I put the ways of childhood behind me. For now, we see only a reflection behind me"** (1 Corinthians 13:11 (NIV).

During my senior year in high school, I came across my oldest sister's longtime friend, named Vicki, in a disco club one night while out on the town. I asked Vicki and her sister, Linda, if it was okay to sit with them at their table. I suspected it would be okay because we all had known each other for many years but lived miles apart in separate towns. We had a ball! We laughed, talked, and danced the night away! It was so much fun that Vicki and I started to get to know each other a little better. The so-called bug had bitten me, and I did not see it coming. We had developed a chemistry that was indescribable! In fact, I felt a way that I had never felt before and nicknamed her Toot. Toot was short for Tootsie Roll, the iconic oblong piece of chewy, chocolate candy that I still love today. Through meeting and getting to know Vicki, I began to understand the meaning of Romans 12:9 (ESV): "***Let love be genuine. Abhor what is evil; hold fast to what is good.***"

It was so indescribable that a year later - when I was 19 years old - I asked Vicki to marry me. However, believing in tradition and possessing such high moral character, Vicki kindly told me that I would have to get her father's permission. Shortly afterward, the day came. I asked Vicki's father, Mr. Willie, for permission. Before he granted permission to marry Vicki, he offered me a shot of his homemade moonshine. I was not an alcohol drinker, but I was not going to risk him not granting me permission to marry his daughter. Therefore, I tightly closed my eyes and quickly downed the shot of moonshine in one swallow like a champ! Mr. Willie nodded his head in the affirmative and verbally gave his permission. Thinking about it now, he tested my love for Vicki. That is, if I could down a shot of his homemade moonshine as quickly as I did, then I was good enough for his daughter. 1 Corinthians 16:14 (ESV) states, "***Let all that you do be done in love.***" That moonshine burned, but I know now that it was Mr. Willie's simple way of discerning whether I would do anything for Vicki. His approval said he knew I would.

My Wife

Currently, Vicki and I have been married for 37 years. During this time, we have gotten to know each other very well: spiritually, emotionally, and mentally. Together, we have traveled and lived many places in the United States and Japan when I was active duty in the military. In fact, three months were the longest and only time we were physically separated from each other. This occurred in 1981 when I first enlisted in the military and consecutively attended the Air Force Basic Military Training and Air Force Law Enforcement Technical School. We have two adult sons and one handsome grandson. Today, I can easily proclaim that I have unconditional love for my wife and family. She has always been a woman of God, and I have grown to love her more each day: both in sickness and in health.

In June 2016, Vicki was diagnosed with Stage 4 metastatic breast cancer, which meant the cancer had spread to other parts of her body. This initially knocked us off our feet. However, we got back up, dust ourselves off, and called on our Almighty God. **Isaiah 41:10 (NIV) states, *"So do not fear, for I am with you; be not dismayed, for I am your God. I will strengthen you and help you. I will uphold you with my righteous right hand."***

While God did a remarkable work with Vicki, I stayed by her side the entire journey. For instance, since the time she started chemo (2016), I attended all her chemo treatments except for three or four because of my work schedule. Each treatment was four hours. I also told Vicki repeatedly that if I had the power to remove the cancer from her body and place it in mine that I would do so in a heartbeat. In fact, the chemo causes much pain to Vicki's toes and fingers, which causes her to moan and groan throughout the night. This tears my heart apart . . . so I constantly offered to rub her feet and hands to give her comfort until she falls asleep. 1 John 4:8 (NIV) states, "***Whoever does not love does not know God, because God is love.***"

Fast forward: On March 31, 2019, Vicki was admitted to the hospital because she had vomited blood. Thinking what was wrong with my baby, I was terrified and rushed her to the emergency room. Her doctor said the endoscopy showed esophageal varices (enlarged veins in the esophagus), but they were not bleeding. This was good news, but the doctor did see some gastritis-irritation of the stomach lining, which probably caused the bleeding. Plus, her blood count was low. A biopsy of both areas (esophagus and stomach lining) was conducted and later revealed there was no new cancer. I praised and thanked the Lord for answering my prayers when she was hospitalized. Moreover, during this five-day stay in the hospital, the only time I left Vicki's bedside was to rush home to shower and shave and then returned to the hospital, which only took 40 minutes. After the five-day stay in the hospital, I have repeatedly told Vicki while in bed how much I love her and gently held her hand until she fell asleep. Ephesians 5:25 (NIV) states, "***Husbands, love your wives, just as Christ loved the church and gave himself up for her.***"

From April 24 to May 14, 2019, Vicki received a 15-day radiation treatment to address the gastritis-irritation of her stomach lining. Upon completion, she experienced several side effects causing her to have a high fever. She visited her doctor, and he prescribed her antibiotics and placed her on a five-day intravenous (IV) treatment. Consequently, I was right there beside her for each treatment. During this time, I cooked or ordered food, cleaned house, did laundry, and helped Vicki get dress for church on Sunday. I really did not want Vicki to do anything but only focus on getting well and serving the Lord. Plus, my marriage vows, stated September 12, 1981, were as follows: "***I, Bobby Lowe, take you, Vicki, to be my wedded wife. To have and to hold, from this day forward, for better, for worst, for richer, for poorer, in sickness or in health, to love and to cherish till death do us part. And hereto I pledge you my faithfulness.***"

Dr. Bobby L. Lowe was born to Robert L. Lowe and Lizzie Lowe in Caledonia, MS, and graduated from Caledonia High School.

He earned a Doctor of Philosophy in Education with a specialization in Leadership in Educational Administration from Capella University. Dr. Lowe is a faithful member at Reaching the Remnant Ministries. He was married to his caring and loving wife, Victory, 37 years. They have two sons, Derrick and Tyler, and one adoring grandson, Dallas. Dr. Lowe is a retiree of the United States Air Force after proudly serving his country for 20 years as a law enforcement specialist. He has worked as a schoolteacher and school administrator at Montgomery Public Schools, Alabama, for 18 years and is currently an online adjunct professor at Concordia University, Ashford University, and University of Phoenix. He also supervises scorers in the edTPA program at Pearson Education. His motto is "You can do all things through God!"

Editor's Epilogue: *On Monday, November 25, 2019, Bobby's beautiful angel and my friend made her transition from time to eternity. Mrs. Victory*

C. Lowe never lost her faith in God's healing power and until her last breath praised Him for her life's journey. In her final moments, just as in the 37 years of their marriage and the years, months, and days of her arduous battle, the love of her life, Bobby, was right there by her side.

Failure Is Not an Option – In God

REV. RAYMONDA R. SPELLER

I grew up on Gospel music. There is something about the feeling you get when listening to a good church choir: the soaring soprano notes and booming baritone voices. I am transported somewhere higher when I hear good Gospel singing. And one of the songs that really does it is "There Is No Failure in God." I love the powerful musical declaration that there is no failure in God! But a part of me wishes that back when I was growing up listening to that powerful song, somebody had written another one that makes it plain that though there is no failure in God, there is absolutely failing moments in people… including in Church.

As I sit in the fifth year of my first senior pastorate, I must admit that I have had some failing moments. There have been moments when I have dropped the ball, felt unwise, missed opportunities, and just come up short. No amount of gifting, anointing, education, prayer, fasting or human wisdom has made me exempt. These failing moments, these experiences when I have been introduced to my own limits and shortcomings, have made the journey of pastoring one full of self-examination and sometimes even sorrow. But those experiences have also created something else in me as a leader and servant: they have taught me how to lean on the One whose legs are sturdier and whose ways are much greater than mine.

The lesson that Apostle Paul gave to the gifted but imperfect Corinthian Church is still true today. It is in our weakness that God's strength is made perfect. Those moments that taste bitter and that furrow our brow and break our hearts, sometimes those moments of weakness and of momentary sorrow teach our hearts to reach out in hope to the One who can catch the falling pieces. Sometimes what we believe is failure is simply that: the pieces falling together. Note that I didn't say falling apart, but "falling together."

Sometimes that sense we get as leaders that things are not going correctly, that our best isn't sufficient, that the vision is not being received, that our limits are halting progress: sometimes what seems like failure is simply God deconstructing what people have pieced together in order to re-create something pure and designed by God. Just because it feels like a failing moment doesn't mean that you are a failure. A season of loss does not mean that all is lost. God has never turned His eyes away and God does not fail, so there is still another season to come. But we have to remember that God is the Lord of the Church and the setter of the seasons. This is God's vineyard, not ours.

Recently, I heard a lecture that will undoubtedly stick with me for a long time. In a symposium for Christian leaders from around the country, a plenary speaker challenged us all to acknowledge that God has not called us to be engineers trying to create a perfectly efficient machine, rather God has called us to be gardeners cultivating a fruitful and faithful Church. The difference is subtle semantically but huge in meaning. An engineer creates, an engineer is the master of her design and creation, an engineer has total power. A gardener just tends the soil and the produce.

The gardener didn't create the seed, doesn't control the quality of the soil, and can't command the rain and sunshine. The gardener just gets up in the morning and trusts that God will do what God does. And the gardener prayerfully and patiently works and waits for God to give the increase. The mark of success for the gardener is not perfection but rather faithfulness, and fruitfulness. It is marked by standing humble and hope-filled in God's presence, remaining faithful to what God has called and tending whatever fruit is produced in God's timing through God's power. No wonder Jesus made it clear that he is the vine and that our job is not to create anything of our own power but rather to remain in Him so that he may bear fruit through and in us.

So failure as we so often define it is not an issue for believers. Not to say that we will always make every mark and that our final weary moment has passed, but it is to say that we are not responsible for much of what we so often obsess over. Crop failure due to drought or excessive sun is not the failure of the farmer. Contrary to what some might believe, failing and issues in the places we serve are not always the fault of the leaders. God has ordained seed time and harvest, reaping and sowing, rainy seasons and dry seasons. Our call is to faithfully till the soil of souls and forever remain connected to the True Vine. There is no failure in that!

Rev. Raymonda R. Speller currently serves as the Senior Pastor of the Community Congregational United Church of Christ in Montgomery, AL. He is married to the beautiful Min. Krystle Speller and they have three young children. His heart's desire is to bring liberation and empowerment to people of all ages and backgrounds through the Word and love of Jesus Christ. Since arriving at CCU, Rev. Speller has been active in community-building work that has impacted the lives of youth and adults alike. His preaching style is both intellectual and passionate, and always brings to light the undiminished truths of the Word of God.

Rev. Speller has earned a Bachelor of Arts degree in Communication and Culture (Speech Communication Emphasis) from Howard University and a Master of Divinity degree from the Duke University Divinity School. He has also done extensive graduate coursework in Leadership and Management.

A community servant at heart, Rev. Speller has been blessed to lead the congregation in expanding its outreach and benevolence ministries exponentially, including now housing the Express-O of Love Diaper and Wipe Bank, offering LIFE (Lifting Individuals and Families to Empowerment) Classes in subjects like financial literacy and anger management, hosting the annual Pink and Pearls for Girls Conference and much more. He is honored to serve on the Board of Directors for the Southeast Conference of the United Church of Christ, the Advisory Council of the Montgomery Community Remembrance Project and as a Clergy Hub Leader of Faith in Action Alabama's Montgomery hub among many other areas of civic and religious service.

Come On, Be Real: Live an Authentic Life!

Marco Mayes

On a glorious Saturday, October 16, 1971, in Tuskegee, Alabama, I arrived to this thing called LIFE! I authentically cried out loud to announce my presence as a bright-eyed African American bouncing baby boy entering a world unbeknownst to me.

It was a world that would not accept me because of the color of my skin. It was a world that would not accept me because of how my voice sounded. It was a world that would not accept me because of how I looked. It was a world that would not accept me because of my intelligence. It was a world that would not accept me because of who I chose to love. It was a world that would not accept me for any chronic disease I acquired. It was simply a world that would not accept me for me being me . . . However, my arrival was met with things from my parents that matched nothing on this planet. Those things were love and fear. They shielded me, comforted me, and fueled my own emotions. So, I have come to realize that my cry for presence . . . was also my cry for acceptance.

At first, I used to question this thing called LIFE and struggled with my existence. I just could not fathom any good in my life outside of my parent's affections. All I knew was that I was the boy that was teased, broken, bullied, mistaken, and misunderstood, nothing else. That was REAL to me! After years of solitude and resentment of myself, the light bulb came on. I remember one day reading, "*There is no fear in love; but perfect love casteth out fear: because fear hath torment. He that feareth is not made perfect in love*" in 1 John 4:18 (KJV). This scripture immediately connected me back to my first authentic cry to this world. I then understood that fear has to exist, but it did not have to live in me, the authentic me! I said, "*Come on Man, Be Real: Live an Authentic Life!*"

Whether you realize it or not, your first authentic cry is the reminder that God Himself created you, loves you, and has never regretted given you the breath to make that first, resounding, unapologetic announcement that you had arrived!

The definition of "authentic" is to be the undisputed origin. To be authentic with yourself, a self-transparency test should be established. Each person must implement what I call the "image triangle" of themselves to measure their originality. There should be a mirror-moment of understanding your mental image, your reflection, and your societal image. First, the "mental image" is what you think you look like in your mind. This image is shaped by personal likes and dislikes. Next, the "reflection" is literally the reflection in the mirror you use to give yourself the once over. This image is shaped by societal likes and dislikes. Then, the "societal image" is how you think another person thinks you look. This image is shaped and powered by personal and societal likes and dislikes. So, the self-transparency test is extremely important.

We as humans often get stuck in the "societal image" phase. Unfortunately, it creates an impractical reality by increasing the likelihood of losing our authentic selves while trying to keep up an image for the benefit of others. This phase thrives specifically on the misplacement of love and fear. The confusion of what is important and realistic blinds individuals into believing what we are thinking is REAL. During this time, an individual can spew hate uncontrollably and not know it. The fake reality of thinking everyone has to look, sound, love, ache, or replicate actions the way we do can be very detrimental in many ways. An unrealistic life is not an authentic life!

I believe God allows love and fear to exist at two very pivotable point in our lives: birth and death! Those times of our lives are closely related and familiar because of these two emotions. Humans inauspiciously gravitate towards needing or dealing with both emotions simultaneously. The newborn has no clue on how to manage them but fearfully and instinctively understands it needs love to feel comfort. The person close to transitioning life has a knowledge base from both emotions but struggles with where to place that love or fear. All are perfectly natural and warranted as being human.

This also proves why humans comfortably and easily attach to those emotions when dealing with any ordeals of living. It is because there is some familiarity with them already. The tricky part in being human is deciding which emotion will take precedent in us. This is the true authentic test! The fine line between these two points make understanding and living life very simple, but societal pressures can make it hard.

Oh wait, you did know God purposely arranged it that way, right? *"For I know the plans I have for you, declares the Lord, plans for the welfare and not for evil, to give you a future and hope"*

Jeremiah 29:11 (KJV). God created the time in between birth and death for you to have the opportunity to LIVE. It was never stated that it would be easy, only mandatory to do. Embrace every moment to be a blessing of hope for every single thing with which you come into contact. Ignore how uncomfortable it makes you and find a comfortable spot to show your blessing. Ignore how unknowledgeable you are with it and find the knowledge to show your blessing. Never miss an embracing moment.

Every human is guaranteed a birth and a death. Your birthday was also the start of your expiration. The actions you take and how you take them with your life before you expire are crucial. Treat and accept every individual they way YOU would like be treated and accepted. That rule means even more when they do not treat you same. The authentic you, quite frankly, should make you do it naturally. The base of that word is "natural" which means it was given to you at birth by God. Never misuse what God has given you. He gave us life for a reason!

What are you doing with your time between birth and death? My goal with that time is simple: I want to be used as much as possible by as many resources available to better someone's life before transitioning. Genuinely and undoubtedly originally! I charge EVERYONE to do the same! Come On, Be Real: Live an Authentic Life!

Marco Antony Mays is an advocate, humanitarian, empowerment speaker, events manager and model. He is the Founder and CEO of M2, a consulting company, specializing in Personal Development and Events Management. He also is the founder of M2 Cares, a humanitarian project created to promote healthy eating and living in small communities. He is highly sought after for his ability to seamlessly create, plan, and execute the ideas and visions of his clients.

He is currently a Brand Ambassador for Until There's A Cure, a non-profit organization focused on ending HIV/AIDS, a Civil Rights/Outreach Specialist for the Central Alabama Fair Housing Center, and a Funeral Director at Brookside Funeral Home & Crematorium. He has appeared in television and big screen works with Wind Creek Casino & Hotel (AL), ATLAS2018 Documentary (Netherlands), Her Vision Studio's Traces of Indignity (2019 Movie), and Model Behavior with Sharon Quinn (NYC). Some projects of his work include "The Brunch with Marco Mays" (USA), "Full Figured Fashion Week" (NYC), Queen Size Magazine, RSVP Montgomery Magazine, "A Taste of Cultures" for Hot Spots (AL), Plus Night Out (NYC), and LS 1426, Inc. (FL), to name a few. He is an active Board member on Colors River Region (LGBT Youth), National Minority AIDS Council (NMAC), Alabama Consumers Advisory Board (ALCAB), Central Alabama Alliance Resource Advocacy Center (CAARAC), and the Veteran's Mental Health Council (LGBT Veterans).

He is currently the Vice-President of Triumph Service's Junior Board. He also sits on the Rosa Parks Museum's Community Givers Junior

Board and the Montgomery Museum of Fine Art's Junior Board. His volunteering spans from local and national community work with Easter Seals, AIDS Alabama, Medical Advocacy & Outreach, Collaborative Solutions Inc., CAVHCS's National Coming Out, Alabama Department of Public Health, for the LGBTQ community. Marco resides in Millbrook, Alabama and holds a Bachelor of Arts in Communication with a concentration in Public Relations from Auburn University at Montgomery.

Growing Pains: In My Weakness, I Found His Strength (Falling into Grace)

REV. BENNIE LIGGINS

*The highway of the upright avoids evil; those who
guard their ways preserve their lives.*
18 Pride goes before destruction, a haughty spirit before a fall.
*19 Better to be lowly in spirit along with the oppressed
than to share plunder with the proud.*
*20 Whoever gives heed to instruction prospers, and blessed is
the one who trusts in the LORD. (Proverbs 16:17-20 NIV)*

January of 2011 brought forward what promised to be a prosperous
and blessed year. Everything seemed to be falling into place. My
wife and I were celebrating three years of marriage, and our blended
family was indeed beginning to blend. In addition, the Lord had
given me a vision for the church and everyone in the congregation
begin to embrace their roles to make our mission statement a
living, viable road map for doing ministry. Life was good. The
church was growing financially, physically, and spiritually. Our
footprint in the community was being enlarged. We were making
a difference. My life could not have been better. Unfortunately,
I was seduced by my success and started to forget that it was not
me but Him. The Lord was about to provide me with a powerful
reminder.

In March of 2011, after what was described as "minor surgery," my heart stopped twice. I literally died twice and was revived each time. I then slipped into a coma for 17 days with the last seven days showing little signs of brain activity. They suggested to my wife on the tenth day that she should just let me go, but she refused. She said, "We walked into this hospital together, and the Lord has shown me that we will walk out together." Thank God for her faith!

On day 17, the Lord woke me up and opened my eyes to an unfamiliar world. I could not see, speak or walk without stumbling. In other words, many of the things that I thought made me an effective pastor and preacher - charisma, command of the English language, stature - were taken away. Whereas people who looked at me with respect, love and envy, now seemed to show only benevolence and pity. I was humbled by eight plus years of recovery that is still in progress. I had to learn how to talk, walk, dress and feed myself again. I was humbled . . . but the journey has and is making me stronger.

> *25 But if we hope for what we do not yet*
> *have, we wait for it patiently.*
> *26 In the same way, the Spirit helps us in our weakness.*
> *We do not know what we ought to pray for, but the Spirit*
> *himself intercedes for us through wordless groans.*
> *27 And he who searches our hearts knows the mind*
> *of the Spirit, because the Spirit intercedes for God's*
> *people in accordance with the will of God.*
> *28 And we know that in all things God works for the*
> *good of those who love him, who have been called*
> *according to his purpose. (Romans 8:25-28 NIV)*

Very arduous and sometimes painful physical, speech and occupational therapy, taught me that I had to lean and depend on Jesus. I was also blessed with an angel, Gloria Liggins, who took a leave of absence from work and never left my side. Through it all, I gained strength from coming to know without a doubt that God is real for I could feel him in my soul. Now I know familiar scriptures in a new and more powerful way.

> *Even though I walk through the valley and shadow of death,*
> *I will fear no evil for you are with me (Psalm 23:17 NIV)*
> *Naked I came in the world and naked I shall depart.*
> *The Lord gives and Lord takes away; blessed*
> *the name of the Lord (Job 1:21 NIV)*
> *I can do all things through Christ who*
> *strengthens me (Philippians 4:13 NIV)*

I am now stronger, wiser, and better thanks be to God. **My report is that Jesus can never be all that you need until He is all that you have.** The Lord was trying to use me in a very special and powerful way, but my pride kept getting in the way. I thought God needed my soaring oratory and persuasive liturgy to reach his people, but I found out that what He really wanted was a willing and submissive servant. I thought of myself more highly than I ought to, and the Lord had to humble me so that he could properly use me.

I remember the first time I stepped in the pulpit about six months after being told I would never preach again. It was a clear evening at the church. The church was full. It seemed that everybody was excited but me. My body was weak. I needed assistance to get into the pulpit. My speech was slurred. I thought my words were hard to understand. In my eyes, I didn't look or sound anything like I wanted to as one of God's spokespersons.

I said, "**Lord, please don't make me do this. This is not the way I want to be seen. This is not how I want to be heard.**" Suddenly I heard the Lord say "This is not about you. It's about My Word." Then I repeated the words of our Lord and Savior, Jesus Christ when he asked "Lord, please let this bitter cup pass from me." But then said, just as The Savior did, "Not my will but Thy will be done." I went on and preached that night from the subject "It's All God." I have been preaching ever since. I cannot tell you the number of people who were encouraged on that very special evening. Not by a powerful charming preacher but a frail, humble servant.

Soren Kickgegaard, an 18th century Danish theologian and philosopher once said that "Pain has a way of getting rid of all pretenses." God used my pain to strip all pretenses. He revealed the doubt that came from the pride I was hiding behind so that I could come into a real relationship with Him. It was only through that genuine connection that people could hear and actualize the words of peace, comfort, and strength that only a true relationship with Jesus can provide.

Consider it pure joy, my brothers and sisters, whenever you face trials of many kinds, because you know that the testing of your faith produces perseverance. Let perseverance finish its work so that you may be mature and complete, not lacking anything. (James 1:2-4 NIV)

I CONCLUDE MY REPORT WITH THIS: I WOULD NOT WISH EVERYTHING THAT HAPPENED UPON MY WORST ENEMY. BUT I AM VERY THANKFUL THAT IT HAPPENED TO ME.

Pastor Bennie Liggins is a native of Memphis, Tennessee. He is a graduate of LeMoyne-Owen College in Memphis, where he received a Bachelor of Science Degree in Economics. He received a Master in Crisis Ministry Degree from Candler School of Theology, Emory University, Atlanta, Georgia and a Master of Divinity from the Interdenominational Theological Center in Atlanta, Georgia

Pastor Liggins has the distinction of serving as the Pastor of all three United Church of Christ in Montgomery, Alabama. Since 2005 he is the founding Pastor of Unity Worship Center. A viable congregation meeting the critical needs of the residents of Montgomery, Alabama. He has also served the church at the conference and national level, when he served as Associate Conference Minister for New Church Starts for the Southeast Conference. In that capacity he aided in the start and/or developments of over 23 churches.

In addition to his civilian ministry, Reverend Liggins served the nation for more than 26 years as an Aviator and a Chaplain in the United States Air Force. His military career includes tours as an Aviator in KC-135 aircraft and a Staff Chaplain. He service was distinguished as Director of the Orientation Course and the Developer of the first Distance Learning Courses of the Chaplain Service Institute, Maxwell Air Force Base, Montgomery, Alabama, and Deputy Chief of Personnel for the United States Chaplain Service. Over the years, his ministry has taken him to every continent. He retired in 1999 at the rank of Lieutenant Colonel.

Selfless service to God is the hallmark of Pastor Liggins' ministry. He loves the Lord and he derives great joy from helping people. Reverend Liggins and his wife Gloria are the proud parents of 5 children and 13 grandchildren.

Be Valiant: If We Build Them, They Will Succeed

ANTHONY BROCK

In my educational journey, God has truly blessed me with the opportunity to help shape the minds of the future generations. Throughout the years, there have been countless opportunities for me to learn just as much from them as they have from me. My prayer is that my impact will last a lifetime as they transition into different phases of their lives. This is a brief story and testimonial about God giving me a vision and then sending provision to carry it out. The provision didn't come without trials and delays along the way, but through it all, God has been faithful.

I am from Montgomery, went to Lanier High School and attended Alabama State University. My brother Fred played football for Jeff Davis, University of Southern Mississippi, and in the NFL for the Arizona Cardinals. After college I began my career in 1999 in Prattville, Alabama. I worked there for over eighteen years with a brief two-year stint in Atlanta. After football, Fred settled in Florida working in commercial development.

I have always had the desire to create change within the students I worked with while they were still at an impressionable age. That process took flight due to an encounter with a student during my routine walk through the halls. This encounter became the final straw and proved to be the strongest motivation for what would manifest as Valiant Cross Academy. The young man was sitting in the hallway with his head tucked in between his legs. As I inquired about why his teacher put him outside of the classroom, I discovered that he was sleeping during instructional time every day. In my conversation with him he disclosed that his lack of attention and energy in class was due to him caring for his younger siblings as his mother worked late at night. At that very moment, God's voice returned to me with a reminder, "Remember what I told you to do!"

I begin a mentoring program in Prattville in 2005 called Brother2Brother and Sister2Sister to spend extra time with my students. The program was started with the sole purpose of molding our male youth to be productive citizens. I spent years taking young people on college trips, orchestrating educational field trips, conducting etiquette training, and teaching these hungry minds how to interview for future job positions. Because of the consistent love and high expectations on the students in the program, they grew to understand and appreciate the program's purpose. The program yielded a lot of fruit. I was eventually able to launch it in three out of the four middle schools in the Autauga County School System.

My career was moving along well as I decided to go back to earn my Master's degree in Educational Leadership. After receiving my degree, I envisioned the road to becoming a principal would be a slow and gradual journey, but everything worked in the God's timing which happened to be a trip on a fast track. I begin to see what it meant in Proverbs 3:6 in stating "***In all thy ways acknowledge him, and he will direct your paths.***" I completed my Master's program at Alabama State University in the spring

2007. During the fall of 2008, I had the pleasure of becoming the head football coach of the Prattville Junior High School. The next few years were full of promotions and an increasing territory. I am humbled to share that when I read the Prayer of Jabeez over fifteen years ago and as I pray it every morning, God continues to hear and answer. The following year, in 2009, I moved into an assistant principal job. In 2010, I was hired at Central Office as the County At-Risk Specialist, and finally moved into a principal job at the Second Chance Program.

Fred and I had always talked about transitioning back to Montgomery to work with young people in our hometown. We felt compelled to stand in the gap and present them with another outlook on life. After a short period of working at Huntington College as an assistant football coach, Fred accepted a job at Saint Jude Educational Institute as the Athletic Director and Head Football Coach. We were excited about this new opportunity for Fred. The idea of us working together would always arise in our talks around St. Jude. That dream only seemed like a dream because I was still working in Prattville, and I had just signed a new three-year contract. Despite the predicament, I still wanted to implement a mentoring program to impact the students at the school. I also wanted to work alongside my brother.

This is the first of two "Fork in the road experiences" in my life...
"Lord, if it's you," Peter replied, "tell me to come to you on the water." Matthew 14:28

The constant voice saying "Go!" that I heard in my prayers was reassurance that I was following the right path. While discussing the impact we could make and after many talks with the director of the school, the dream was finally made a reality as an opportunity presented itself. Through many sessions of prayer and countless consultations with my wife, I resigned from my position and accepted the principal job at St. Jude Educational Institute in the Fall of 2013. If you want to walk on water, you must get out the boat. I literally jumped out of the boat and found myself in uncharted waters!

During our time at St. Jude Educational Institute, Fred and I felt things were really going well. We were looking to increase the enrollment and put a lot of effort into rejuvenating the parents and alumni. We upgraded the technology by installing a smart board into the school and a television in every classroom. We excelled in creating a positive school culture as well as experiencing the continued success of St. Jude's athletic program. Despite the victories in the school and with the athletic program, the movement was short lived. The school came to an unexpected close in May 2014.

The second major "Fork in the road experience" was about to take place. "Delight yourself in the Lord and He will give you the desires of your heart." Psalms 37:4

For years I can remember this dream of opening an all-male school. I've longed for an institution where I could start from scratch and implement the philosophies and ideals that I believed in and knew would be life-changing for the young men who came through its doors. I am thoroughly convinced that the Lord had heard my prayers through the years, but that He was waiting for His perfect timing. Many people want to be used for the glory of God, but there are times in which we must experience humility.

The closing of St. Jude was a moment of humility that propelled me into my purpose. The seeds that I had planted over the course of my educational journey were about to bear ripe fruit. We were able to form a board to entertain the purpose of opening a school. We decided along with our board to take one year to plan a school that I believed would change the course of education throughout the country.

We opened **VALIANT CROSS ACADEMY** in 2015 and currently serve 6th through 10th-grade young men with each grade matriculating up until they graduate. The Academy is a private school built on Christian principles with an intentional culture of structure and discipline. We have distinctive uniforms, an effective consequence and award system, and an intense focus on the academic success of our scholars. Our academic program includes small class sizes, longer school days, differentiated instruction, and aggressive tutoring. Our vision is to prove that there is not an achievement gap amongst minorities, but rather an opportunity gap. We believe with Christ, consistency, and high expectations, that these young men will be successful.

Valiant Cross Academy provides a loving, stable educational opportunity for young men in Montgomery, Alabama. We believe in developing leaders by teaching each one of our scholars the necessary skills to become productive citizens, leaders in the community, and honorable men. If we build them, they will succeed.

The Valiant Cross Academy Creed

The world does not need supermen. It needs supernatural men.
Men who will learn from their youth, to let go of self, to let the
power of the Holy Spirit raise them to new heights. Courageous
men, righteous men, committed men, loving men who will rise
up to lead, to serve, and to inspire.

We are Valiant Cross Academy.
Our mission, our purpose, our promise
is to help raise up such men.
The foes are formidable. But our God is mighty.
We are Valiant Cross Academy.
We will provide the armor to help them rise above.
To rise above with Honor. To rise above with Discipline.
To rise above with Integrity. To rise above with Excellence.
To rise above with Love.
We are Valiant Cross Academy.
In this place, young men will Rise Above.

Anthony Brock is a native of Montgomery and is married to D'Tanja Brock with whom he shares two beautiful daughters, Noah and Jonah.

He is an active member of St. Paul A.M.E. Church where he serves as a Steward, Men's Usher, Men's Chorus Member, and Young Adult Sunday School Teacher. He is a proud member

of Kappa Alpha Psi Fraternity, Inc. Mr. Brock also serves on the Alabama Leadership Council for the Alabama Opportunity Scholarship Fund and the Board of Directors at the Southeast Y.M.C.A. in Montgomery & Prattville Y.M.C.A. His mentoring program was recognized as the Autauga County Service Organization of the Year. The Montgomery alumni chapters of Delta Sigma Theta and Kappa Alpha Psi recognized him as the 2016 Citizen of the Year, and the First Congregational Church in Montgomery recognized him and his brother with the "2016 Daring to Make a Difference Award." He was selected at the Alabama Black Achievers Gala sponsored by Regions Bank in Birmingham as the Entrepreneur of the Year. Most recently, he was selected by the Alabama Power Company as an Alabama Bright Light, the Troy University and the ASU-Troy University "Martin Luther King Jr. Beloved Community" Award, and he was also selected to ASU's "50 under 50" Inaugural Alumni Class.

"Try Before You Pry"

OVERSEER THOMAS D. TUCKER, IV

I want to establish this from the very beginning: faith is the key that God uses through our prayers to cause doors to open for us. *"And I will give you the keys of the kingdom of heaven: and whatever you bind on earth will be bound in heaven, and whatever you loose on earth, will be loosed in heaven"* (Matthew 16:19 NKJV). I've been walking with and pursuing the Lord for over half of my life. More often than not, I am still amazed at how He uses where I am and what I'm going through to teach me more about who He is. Such is true in the lesson of **TRY BEFORE YOU PRY.**

Back in the early 90s, I was stationed at a place called *Torrejón* Airbase in Spain. I was in the early part of my Air Force career as a firefighter. I served in this career for the duration of my 20-year military career. It was through fire protection that I learned the concept **TRY BEFORE YOU PRY.** This was one of the earlier things that we learned. It seems like a simple concept and one that everyone would logically consider when it comes to rescuing someone trapped in a burning building. The "try before you pry" standard taught us this: **before you use any tools of forcible entry to open a door, you should first try to open the door as you normally would. Turn the doorknob or handle.**

We firefighters love to use manual and power tools to force entry! It's adventurous, spectacular, and dramatic. We find any excuse to use axes, saws, the jaws of life, and other special tools in order to gain entry to doors difficult to open. And while there are times when forcible entry is needed and necessary, many times if we try before we pry, we can save ourselves a whole lot of trouble. Those who pry first are usually faced with two outcomes: they expend tireless effort to accomplish an unneeded objective or they cause unnecessary damage due to a lack of patience.

In this Christian life, we're often like myself and many of my fellow former and active first responders. We become so focused on making the rescue until we use more force than necessary sometimes. *We use forcible means to carry out God's plan rather than using His methods to carry out His plan.* The results can be the same as I learned in fire protection. If we fail to seek God first but go prying instead, the outcome turns into some exhaustive effort only because we failed to seek God first. We are reminded in Proverbs 3:5-7 NKJV, it's always best to *"trust in the Lord with all your heart and lean not to your own understanding. In all your ways acknowledge Him, and He will direct your path."* There are countless areas in my life that, because I did things my way, ended in disaster just as promised in Proverbs 14:12 NKJV – *there is a way that seems right unto a man, but the end thereof are the ways of death.* There are many doors we try to open on our own. But if we would *"try before we pry"* and allow God to deliver on the promises in His Word, doors would open as He intends with no fruitless effort and unnecessary damage on our part!

I was married with two children at *Torrejón*, and we would soon have one on the way. I was a "two-striper," which meant I didn't have a whole lot of money. It was the month of June and we were eagerly expecting the arrival of our third child. We were already blessed with having two beautiful girls, so you can imagine that our prayers would be that God bless us with our baby boy when the time came. It was finally time to deliver this child that we had been eagerly anticipating. God blessed us with another baby almost 8 pounds full of energy and full of life. This baby was everything that we envisioned it to be except "he" was "she." Yes, another girl! From the moment this child entered the world she completely captured my heart. But was one major concern for her mother and me: she had a serious birth defect. How can I explain it? Imagine how our legs normally flex at the knee backwards. Torie's legs flexed from the knees forward.

My wife and I were scared of course, but for some reason, there was also a calm that God allowed me to have. It was as if I could hear the words of Moses - as he faced the Red Sea, had the Pharaohs army to his back, the waters before him, and the mountains on the side of him – saying "stand still and see the salvation of the Lord" (Exodus 14:13 NKJV). That's the Word God gave me in that instance. That was the way He delivered the ***try before you pry*** message concerning our sweet little baby. Later, some doctors from the University of Madrid arrived. They had seen nothing like this before, but they had come with a master plan. The solution was to set our baby's legs in partial casts every couple of weeks. When each period elapsed, they would reset the cast and keep up this process until Torie's legs were healed.

After the first two weeks, we met these doctors from Madrid in the hospital expecting to them to take her legs out of the cast and then reset them in a different position. But if I tell you God is a healer, you better believe me! Much to our surprise and great joy,

Torie would no longer require any more cast because the Lord healed her legs turning them in the correct position. And she's been walking, running, climbing, and praising God ever since! What Torie's healing and so many other miracles have taught me is that with God, it is our FAITH that opens the doors that we pray about. It's not our prying or trying to force things to happen. In that situation, I was scared and desperately needed God to move for our daughter and us. Therefore, I went straight to God, and only to God because He had all the answers. I had none. As a result, things just worked out accordingly.

After serving as a firefighter by trade 20 years in the Air Force, *try before you pry* has proven to be a valuable lesson professionally and in life. Forcible entry tools, while they are incredible, powerful, and fun, can cause unneeded suffering and damage in the long run. Refuse to delay the will and blessing of God for your life by insisting that you seek God first and do everything His way rather than your own. Ask Sarah, Abraham's wife: when you choose to do things your way rather than His, you will be forced to live with the results (Genesis 21). It may seem ideal in the beginning, but it takes a while at times to comprehend just how much it will cost you in the long run! Have you ever moved without consulting God? It can be so very destructive and cause years of delay toward your destiny. This type of carelessness causes the destruction of marriages, families, finances, ministries . . . Shall I keep going?

I was able to execute such tremendous faith at the birth of my child only because I was desperate. I recognized that we needed God. So what about now? What happens when it seems that I'm capable of accomplishing so much on my own? Those are the times I pray all the more! Listen: every time we start addressing our lives with our own manual power tools, we end up grossly delaying the divine move of God in our lives, or we make a mess of things that only God is able to repair. **TRY BEFORE YOU PRY** assumes that you might eventually have to use tools at some point. I suggest to you that you quit prying altogether because we serve a promise keeping God. Refuse to do things your own way and turn it over completely to the Lord. Do keep on **TRYING** God though! **Try** Him in your home. **Try** Him on your job. **Try** Him in your ministry. **Try Him** and allow God to prove Himself to YOU.

Overseer Thomas Tucker was born at Maxwell AFB, AL, but would grow up to know Colorado Springs, Colorada, as hometown graduating from Widefield High School. Fathering his four children, Terri, Taylor, Torie, and Titus, is his most valued accomplishment. He is also blessed to have 5 beautiful grandchildren: Carter, Skyy, Makenzie, Emory, and Ethan.

Thomas served 20 enlisted in the United States Air Force serving tours of duty in Colorado, Spain, Germany, Florida, Honduras, Saudi Arabia, and South Korea retiring at the rank of Master Sargent. He was called to Gospel Ministry in 1990 and has been serving the Lord ever since. Thomas has been called to preaching from the simplicity of the Gospel that everyone might be able to receive it. He served in the Full Gospel Baptist Church Fellowship International as Director of Evangelism in Florida and Director of Armorbearers for the Southern Atlantic Region. Thomas was elevated to the office of Overseer at Covenant on April

9, 2017. He currently serves as State Overseer of Alabama/Northwest Florida for Kingdom Connection Fellowship International.

Thomas worked for Lockheed Martin as a Firefighter/Inspector in Marietta, Georgia, and he also worked for the Florida Department of Economic Opportunity as a Veterans Outreach Program Specialist, and now he currently serves with the Department of Veteran Affairs as a Veterans Outreach Program Specialist. Thomas serves as a member of the Northwest Florida Panhandle Committee, coordinating Marketing and Social Media. He has earned a Bachelor of Science in Workforce Education and Development through Southern Illinois University, and Master of Divinity, Theology through Liberty Theological. Overseer Tucker is currently pursuing a Master of Social Work from Walden University.

Why Black Men Should Vote

ANDERSON T. GRAVES II

For my ancestors, manhood was not a matter of age but a matter of responsibility to the community. A boy was only considered Man when he completed rites of passage which tested his ability to contribute to the stability and success of the tribe or village. Even then, "manhood" was conditional for a thief, a coward, a slacker who neglected his family. A man who refused his responsibilities in and to the community was a disgrace, an outcast. In the eyes of the community he was no longer a Man.

The most public, i.e., the most civic, expression of earned manhood was the council of elders or the village council. The village council confirmed chiefs, affirmed griots and shamans, settled disputes, meted justice, and set the rules of life in the community. Only men, certified, bonafide MEN, had the right to speak in this circle. Having a voice in village council was the ultimate privilege and a civic responsibility. A man who refused to sit with the elders, a man who consistently neglected the gatherings of the council without very good reason was a slacker, a disgrace. In the eyes of the community, he was not a Man anymore. The Apostle Paul explained to a young leader, "if anyone does not provide for his own, and especially for those of his household, he has denied the faith and is worse than an unbeliever" (1 Timothy 5:8).

Old Testament Israel "cast lots" to set municipal boundaries (Joshua 18 - 21), to assign leadership roles in the house of worship (1 Chronicles 24-26), to choose leaders for tribal representatives (Nehemiah 11: 1-2), and to decide certain questions and controversies (1 Samuel 14: 37-45). Casting lots was like drawing straws or pulling names from a hat. The people trusted God to intervene and direct the outcome. Though the process was outwardly random, all the men in the relevant community were present. In the Bible, being a man meant that you participated in the voting process even when you can't statistically control or predict the outcome. Even in the wake of Jesus' Ascension into Heaven, when the apostles chose Judas' replacement, they "gave forth their lots" in a process many scholars interpret to have been nomination and voting we would recognize today (Acts 1:26). All the apostles participated in the election because it was their duty to their risen Savior.

Today in America, we choose the chiefs of our government, select the judges, sheriffs, and district attorneys who define justice and modify the fundamental rules of the constitution by voting. Voting is a right not available to every member of the community. It is that mark of full citizenship, i.e. Manhood. Sometimes the outcome of the vote isn't what we want or expect. Sometimes the process seems arbitrary or rigged. But that still doesn't change our responsibility.

What our ancestors did in the village council, we do in the voting booth. In America, the right to vote is the defining expression of full citizenship. Franchisement is the mark of civic Manhood. As the sons of our ancestors, as the people of God's covenant, as followers of Jesus Christ - as MEN - we who have the right also bear the responsibility to show up and cast our lots, to show up and take our seat in the council of citizens, to show up and VOTE. A Black man who can vote but doesn't is abdicating his civic power to whatever kinds of men do vote. A Black man who doesn't vote is neglecting his seat at the adult table of civic action and volunteering to be treated like a child whose good is decided by others.

In a December 1, 2016, article titled "Donald Trump Will Be President Thanks to 80,000 People in Three States" the Washington Post stated that Donald Trump won the electoral college by carrying the states of Michigan, Pennsylvania and Wisconsin. "Trump won those states by 0.2, 0.7 and 0.8 percentage points, respectively — and by 10,704, 46,765 and 22,177 votes. Those three wins gave him 46 electoral votes; if [Hillary] Clinton had done one point better in each state, she'd have won the electoral vote, too." White voter turn-out was exceptionally high in 2016, but enough Black people didn't vote in key states in 2016 to have potentially changed the outcome of the Presidential election. On average, Black voter turn-out in Michigan, Pennsylvania and Wisconsin was down 13%. The idea that voting doesn't matter is a lie. It is a lie to trick us into surrendering our civic power to multiply the power of those who do not share our best interests.

Yes, sometimes voting feels like casting random lots. Sometimes the majority in your district is gerrymandered to override the interests of your community. But the gathering of citizens in the council of elders that is your local polling station is still the place where Men are needed. Whether you like the outcome or not, your responsibility is to take your place with the other certified, bonafide citizens who have passed the rite of passage, i.e. voter registration, and to make your vote speak on behalf of your community.

Some people would have you believe that not voting and using every other political tool in the system is somehow more "spiritual." First, look carefully and you'll see those people being very political when it comes to their interests and the interests of their community. It's a new version of Ole Massuh telling Slave Willie that God doesn't want him worrying about money and clothes while Massuh is planning to sell Willie's children down the river so he can by new furniture for the big house. Your community deserves no less than the effort of every vote and ounce of political weight you can organize to move your people forward.

The Apostle Paul advised Christians under Roman rule, "Let every soul be subject to the governing authorities. For there is no authority except from God, and the authorities that exist are appointed by God. Therefore, whoever resists the authority resists the ordinance of God, and those who resist will bring judgment on themselves" (Romans 13: 1-2). When his life and freedom were threatened by the council of elders (Acts 23: 20, 21), the same Paul exercised his full rights and voice as a citizen of Rome in defense of his interests and the interests of his community, the church (Acts 25: 11, 12). This isn't a contradiction. It's a clarification.

A Christian's submission to governing authority is not acceptance of the status quo. It is not meekly bearing one's back to whatever whips past voting majorities have fashioned. Biblical submission to authority means standing up inside the system and using every tool within that system to fight for justice and the prosperity of your community. The fundamental tool in the American system is the vote. So vote.

> Vote because it is the ancestral heritage of Manhood.
> Vote because it is the Biblical tradition of civic life.
> Vote because you can when so many others cannot.

Vote because it is the logical response of
members of any democratic community.
Vote because the other people vote.
Vote because your vote is more powerful
than they want you to believe.
Vote because of the example the apostles
set in the New Testament.
Vote: Because that's what real Men do.

Rev. Anderson Graves, II graduated from Bassfield High School in
Mississippi in 1989 and earned his Bachelor's in Language Education
and Master's in Education
Administration from Alabama State
University. He taught English,
reading, and drama for 11 years
then served as a high school assistant
principal from 2006-2013. In 2006,
Anderson surrendered to the
ministry and now serves pastor of
Miles Chapel CME Church and
Executive Director of SAYNO
(Substance Abuse Youth Network
Organization), a nonprofit to help
youth avoid drugs. He met his wife
Sheila (Asberry) in at Alabama State

University. They have been married 22 years. She is a teacher and the
daughter of a teacher and a principal. They have two children, Kaitlin
and Anderson Graves III.

Train Up a Child: What Black Men Must Teach Their Sons

Dr. Carl Shamburger, Jr.

Let me start this by saying that I love my sons. They keep me going and motivated with an energy that I thought I didn't have. As of today, I still feel disbelief that I was a part of their creation! I can remember the days and times before their birth when I focused on my dreams, what I would eat, and what I was going to do for that day. I did not realize how much time I had on my hands. After their birth, I experience a constant feeling of "I cannot fail because they are dependent on me."

I remember growing up in a little rural town called Pine Hill, Alabama, where everyone knew everyone, and anyone could become your parent if they saw you getting into trouble. I remember powerful men that had an integral part in my life and how they acted in certain circumstances. I even wonder to myself, "How did they feel when they had their sons?" "How did my dad feel when he had me?" From my recollections of seeing the blueprint drawn by my father, I thought of these core principles that I know I must teach my sons.

GOD

First and foremost, we must teach our sons that God exists. We must teach and instill the knowledge that Jesus Christ died for our sins, and that they must be born again. Our sons must know that there is a higher power to which they will answer one day. There is someone that loves them beyond comprehension. More than my father does me and I do my sons. We must actively take our sons to church to provide the foundation for them spiritually. I remember growing up and attending church every Sunday with my family. My father made it his priority to wake us up and get us to church. He would also often go by himself if we did not get up in time.

I can be honest to say that when I left home after graduating from high school, I did not attend church regularly. I went to college at Alabama A&M University and lived based on the mantra "work hard, lay hard". As I progressed through life, things began to get tougher. My coursework began to get more demanding. I had to grow up. I found myself needing help, needing answers for life's questions, and needing rejuvenation. I began to attend church more regularly. I began to take notice of the many times in my life when God had stepped in for me. It was the knowledge of God that was instilled in me as a child that kept me on the right path. Black men should make this a priority for our sons. Proverbs 22:6 KJV says *Train up a child in the way he should go; even when he is old, he will not depart from it.* Our sons, because of our example, must feel confident and comfortable in worshipping God and know they can pray and talk with God for themselves at any time.

LOVE

Love is a very powerful word. It is an emotion that can embody many other emotions and have a ripple effect on all who are involved. Black men must love their sons like God loves us. Within love there are several traits that germinate such as compassion for all people, empathy for those who are troubled, care for the sick, and support for friends and family. If our sons can love someone, they can help someone. I truly believe God wants us to help others here on earth, and He will take care of us in the process. I also believe that helping others requires that we are giving of things needed from us. I want my sons to give their time to people they love, try to help the church, and people in need. We saw Jesus exhibit this love throughout the New Testament. Humans cannot survive without love. 1 John 4:8 says *Anyone who does not love does not know God, because God is love.* If we love our sons and they know how to exhibit that love in various ways to others, it will blanket a lot of their shortcomings. Since God is love, it can conquer anything our sons face in life. There is no way we can forget to teach them this.

RESPECT

A black father should teach his sons to have a myriad of respect. Young boys and men need to know the importance of having respect for everyone. Respect for women in the sense that women are to be protected and treated as equals in society. They should look to help women by being polite and doing things such as opening doors for them. Chivalry is not dead. We all have a story and culture as well as a voice to be heard. Respect for the elderly is absolutely necessary because they have lived here longer than us and have great wisdom. Our sons should have great patience and attention when it comes to the elderly. 1 Peter 5:5 ESV says *Likewise, you who are younger, be subject to the elders. Clothe yourselves, all of you, with humility toward one another, for "God opposes the proud but gives grace to the humble."* Our sons should also have respect for us, their parents. Exodus 20:12 KJV says *"Honor your father and your mother, that your days may be long in the land that the Lord your God is giving you."*

Let me talk a bit about an area of respect that is especially crucial for black males: respect for authority and police. Now this point is important. I have been pulled over by the police for no reason at all. One particularly unnerving experience took place while I was attending the University of Alabama at Birmingham School of Dentistry in 2009. I was leaving my classmate's home around 10:00 P.M after studying all evening and was pulled over. After stopping and looking out the rearview, I noticed I was pulled over by 3 cop cars and they all had their weapons unsheathed and in hand.

As one of the cops approached my window, he announced for me to keep my hands visible. I followed all the officer's directions and politely asked why I was pulled over. I was told there was a report of a stolen vehicle like the Jeep Grand Cherokee that I owned. I was then asked why I was in the neighborhood and when I told the police the truth, I was forced to call my classmate to confirm what his address was. Sad to say this wasn't my first time being pulled over. However, I gave the officers respect despite knowing I may have not done anything wrong. In current American culture, our sons must know that disrespect to authority and the police can be the difference between life and death.

Ultimately our sons must respect themselves. They must know that they represent themselves, their family, and their community wherever they go. They should take care of their physical bodies as well as mental health. Physical appearance should be up kept. I was taught that you only get one first impression and our sons need to make sure that the first impression is their best one.

INTEGRITY

The Webster dictionary defines integrity as "a firm adherence to a code of especially moral or artistic values, and the quality or state of being complete or undivided." I was taught that you must be the same person every day and not "flip flop." Having good moral character and the ability to do the right thing when no one is watching is not always easy. Black men should teach their sons to have high moral character and exhibit this character throughout all walks of life. For example, when their teacher is not looking at them, they should still follow the rules of the class. If they have been told to complete a task, they should want to complete it without having to be constantly pressed. There should be a level of honesty with everything that they do. Being transparent and honest will help our sons be more productive and efficient members in society. Proverbs 12:22 NIV says *The LORD detests lying lips, but he delights in people who are trustworthy.* There is nothing good about a person who lies and does not uphold their end of the bargain. Our sons must know this and feel compelled to hold high the things they are required to do as model citizens.

RESILIENCE

As a black man in America, I have felt the harshness of negative stereotypes that we face. I have walked in public places and seen people grab their children as in what seems like fear. I have noticed others walk very awkwardly to avoid my presence. Sometimes I might be ignored and not seen at all. Black men should teach their sons about these realities and prepare them by making them resilient. Our sons must be tough! When I say tough, I know physical stature and prowess comes to mind and that is great to have, but they must also have mental fortitude.

There will be many roadblocks along our sons' paths, and there will be times when they fail at things they attempt. Sometimes they will fail because of not having the ability yet or because of a reason out of their control. It is in these times that they must know to get up and try again. Their minds cannot falter and become brittle to failure or being categorized. Subsequently they must return even stronger than before with a determination to succeed. They should not focus on the amount of times they were knocked down but on the times the door of opportunity was opened after getting up.

BE YOUR BEST SELF

We must also teach our sons to do the best they can in whatever endeavors they pursue. There is no room for them to be mediocre or lackluster in their performance. Our sons must know that even in the simplest of tasks, they should take pride in it and do it their best. They must experience the comfort in knowing that you gave it your all in doing something even if you fell short of the prize. I was taught that if I can't do my best work, then I shouldn't do it at all. I have learned that teaching this can be better when using a reward system. When we see our sons do their best, we must reward and acknowledge that. There is immense power in a father's approval. Being their best self also applies to our sons' attitudes and physical presentation. If our sons always have a positive attitude, are comfortable in who they are, and present themselves and their works at their best, they will have a higher probability of success and self-satisfaction.

STEWARDSHIP

We must teach our sons to be financially responsible as well as good stewards of God's gifts and talents that were given to them. In my parents' household, education was the answer to everything. My mother worked in the school system for over 40 years holding various positions from teacher to superintendent, and she made it known that by having a college degree, you increase your chances of having a career to make an honest living. My father in turn would always say, "But you have to manage that money. You can't spend every dime you get." I had chores growing up to earn an allowance and periodically my parents would drive me to the store for me to pick out a toy with my own money.

I learned how to save money for a goal and that I had to work for it. It wasn't until college that I fully grasped the concepts my father tried to teach about money as far as financial responsibility. When you run out of money in college, it is not a good feeling. There are so many of us who do not know how to budget, save for a rainy day, have bad spending habits, spend money on things that lose value or are not necessities, and wonder why we are always in a rut financially. Let's give our sons a fighting chance by teaching them the tools that will give them an edge financially.

As a father, I often feel that I am not sure if what I am doing is right for my sons. I know they have a purpose here on earth. I wish I knew what that purpose was so I could help propel them to it. I want only the best for my sons. I am sure my father felt the same about me. So allow me to conclude with this message for all fathers:

We must have a positive and immovable presence in our sons lives. Our sons learn so much from us by what we do on a daily basis, from how we treat our wives, treat other people, and handle life's curves. I know this is true because the majority of what I learned as a man was from being a witness of my father being one. We must first seek counsel from God and internalize the concepts discussed to have a consistent presence in their lives. If we are there in a meaningful, active, consistent way, our sons will grow and thrive. We will not have all the answers. Our methods may not always prove successful. But our presence in our son's lives is crucial to aiding them to become the men God has created them to be.

Dr. Carl M. Shamburger, Jr. is a graduate of Wilcox Central High School where he was the Valedictorian. After high school he pursued an undergraduate degree in Chemistry at Alabama Agricultural & Mechanical University and graduated Summa Cum Laude. He then attended the University of Alabama at Birmingham School of Dentistry, where he graduated among the top of his class. Carl has received awards from the American Academy of Esthetic Dentistry, the Academy of

Operative Dentistry, the Academy of General Dentistry, the American College of Dentists, and from the UAB School of Dentistry Department of Periodontics. He is a member of the American Dental Association, the Alabama Dental Association, the National Dental Association, and the Academy of General Dentistry. Dr. Shamburger is dedicated and motivated to provide quality dental care to the community. He currently is part owner with his wife, Dr. Dominique Shamburger of Montgomery Dental Arts. When not in the office, Dr. Shamburger enjoys spending time with his family – including sons Carl III, Caleb, and Clay - friends, and sports.

A Noise in the Bushes: God Always Has a Plan

REV. WARRICK E. MAYE

"It's beginning to look a lot like Christmas everywhere you go . . ." The words of Meredith Wilson's 1951 musical ode to the season are probably familiar to you. Indeed, the all-encompassing holiday season that runs from Thanksgiving through the New Year is characteristically filled with music playing and everyone rejoicing. We become consumed with thoughts of shopping, giving & receiving gifts, and family gatherings. The struggle often becomes remembering that the true reason for the season is to celebrate the birth of the Savior of the world, Jesus Christ. What a wonderful time it is as we prepare to *"go tell it on the mountain that Jesus Christ is born!"*

I want to share my story of the Christmas day in 1972 that would change my life forever and at the same time send me down the path to God's destiny for my life. *Oh What a Beautiful Morning, Oh What a Beautiful Day* it was that the five of us – me at age 3, my mother, my father, and 1-year-old brother, and Grandma. We had traveled from Mobile, Alabama, to Grandma's home in Frisco City and were traveling to Pensacola, Florida, to celebrate Christmas with so many loved ones. We were traveling the roads that were more than familiar to the adults. We stopped by my dad's my house for a few moments, and my Uncle Charles decided to ride to Shiloh with the family.

But then he began to think about his chore for the morning: washing clothes before his mother got back from the store! Uncle Charles asked my Dad to turn around and take him back to the house at Brooks Farm on Highway 21 outside of Red Hill. My mother, Joyce, was a brand new graduate of Alabama A&M University who had just completed her first semester as a teacher. Dad, Calvin Eugene, was working in Atlanta to provide for his family. With a young family, they both understood and appreciated spending time with their large, extremely close extended families.

Traveling from one home to another during the holidays was just a natural thing for them, and they wanted their children to know the joys of family and to hear the sounds of laughter brought on by precious shared memories. Little did Joyce & Calvin know . . . this would be their last time to pass the tradition down. After dad dropped off Uncle Charles, we headed toward Shiloh. We didn't make it though. At the top of the hill out of nowhere, there was a vehicle driving in the middle of the road. It hit our car head-on and split it in half.

I'm told that within minutes people began to gather around, and word spread of a terrible car accident on the highway. Police officers and paramedics arrived and did their best to keep people away from the scene. In the aftermath and devastation of the wreck, my mother Joyce, my father Calvin, my grandmother Ida Mae, and little brother Derrick were all assumed to be deceased. The police officers reported, "It's a tragic accident, and I don't think we have any survivors." With his last few breaths, my father Calvin was heard saying, "Help, Help!" Those gathering around the site, including friends and family, tried to help, but the police officer said, "Stay away until the coroner gets here!" Upon a search for pulses, they found three bodies lifeless and one with a faint heartbeat. But thank God for an elderly white couple standing in the crowd who said, "Sir, I think there is movement and a noise in the bushes . . ."

And yes, there was certainly a body in the bushes. It was badly injured with two broken legs, a broken arm, and a broken jawbone, BUT IT STILL HAD LIFE. That noise in the bushes was coming from me. God had saved my life from the wreck that would eventually take everyone else in the vehicle. I was transported from the bushes to Monroeville Hospital, and they immediately said, "He needs to be transported to Mobile General Hospital by ambulance." But the owner of Wolff Ambulance Service refused to transport without $300 from my family who was devastated. It is Sunday and Christmas Day. Rather than enjoying family dinners, exchanging gifts, and celebrating, the day turned into a day of mourning. My grandfather couldn't believe the ambulance service would not transport me without the payment! He reached into his pockets and pulled out $300 from monies from moonshine sales and said, "Take him to Mobile!" Many had ridiculed him for his side hustle, but I for one am glad for it!

The nurse needed assistance for the 2-hour ride to Mobile. My uncle Charles, only 17 at the time, had to take the ride with the medic, the driver, and one nurse. He jumped in the ambulance and held up my blood bag as the nurse did all she could to keep me alive. *I know it was the blood that saved me. One day when I was lost, He died on the cross. I know it was the blood that saved me.* That fateful day, it was my uncle Charles, a nervous teenager who could have been in the car during the accident, that helped to save me as he held my blood bag. Halfway to Mobile, the nurse said, "We are not going to make it. Pull in at the hospital in Bay Minette." There was a skeletal staff because of the Christmas holiday. BUT GOD!

A young man – unidentified to this day, an unsung hero from that hospital - jumped in the ambulance and took the remaining ride to help keep my broken body functioning until we arrived in Mobile. Once we arrived, Drs. Leo and Gun told my family, "It looks pretty bad and if he survives . . . he we never walk on his own." *And He walks with me and He talks with me and tells me I am His own!* I am here today as a walking, talking, living, breathing testimony that if God is with you, He can overrule every prognosis. He can take the "Noise in the Bushes" and make him a voice for the Master!

After the tragedy, the word traveled very quickly in the small towns where everyone knew everyone. Christmas was changed for so many people. The newspaper headlines read 3 KILLED ON CHRISTMAS DAY. There was five of us – my mother, father, and grandmother were declared dead there on highway 21. My sweet one-year-old brother survived but died the day of their funeral. The funeral home said they would not have time to pick him up and prepare his body to be buried with everyone else. My granddaddy said, "We can't have another funeral. We can't go through this again. I will go get him." He drove to Mobile and picked up my dear baby brother putting him in the truck, so all four bodies laid in the church together for the funeral service. When the burial plots were prepared, there were five. Only four bodies were in the church and someone said, "There is one survivor - broken up, bruised, by himself, an orphan. It will be a little while . . . and we will bury him too . . ." BUT GOD! *God specializes and He will do what no other power – Holy Ghost power – can do!*

God has said, "I left one here to tell the story," so I open 2020 telling you that the 5th burial spot is still waiting on me behind the Shiloh Baptist Church – where I now serve as senior pastor. I offered my initial sermon at Shiloh on March 28, 1991, because God said, "Tell the story. Tell them as long as there is noise enemy can't destroy you!"

I am that noise in the bushes that has gone on through life with a limp and testimony. That noise in the bushes Graduated Excel High School 1987. Yes, that noise in the bushes got a BS degree from Alabama State 1993. That noise in the bushes went back and got his masters from ASU in 1996. That noise in the bushes continued and got his education specialist degree from ASU in 2006. Yes, that noise in the bushes has done doctoral work at Capella University. That noise in the bushes has served as pastor for 24 years at Westside Baptist Church in Evergreen, Alabama. Yes, that noise in the bushes preaches under the power of the Holy Spirit to tell others about the Ram in the bush! That noise in the bushes encourages other when he sings *the Lord will make a way somehow.* Yes, that noise in the bushes shares with conviction that God will be mother, father and brother.

THIS NOISE IN THE BUSHES – also known as Rev. Warrick Eugene Maye – proclaims that God will heal you, He'll deliver you, and He'll set you free! Yes, this noise in the bushes is a living testimony who's report declares *there is no secret to what God can do. What He's done for others, He'll do for you.*

Rev. Warrick E. Maye is a 1987 graduate of Excel High School. He later attended Patrick Henry Jr. College (Alabama Southern) and Bishop

State Community College. In 1993, he received his Bachelor of Science degree in Social Studies from Alabama State University. In 1996, he received his Master of Education and Education Specialist degrees from Alabama State University. In the summers of 1993 and 1994 he served as missionary in Dermott, Arkansas which was assigned by National Baptist U.S.A. Incorporated. Previously, he was certified through the National Baptist Convention as a certified instructor. He has furthered his studies through Selma University, Montgomery Bible Institute and the University of Mobile.

In 2013 he served as Keynote Speaker for Citizens United for Atmore, 2010 speaker for the MLK Program and Black History Speaker for Fountain Correctional Facility. He was the 2011 recipient of the Spirit of Dr. King Award from Evergreen District Congress. He has been selected Who's Who Among Educators, members of CLAS Organization and Alabama Education Association.

Maye has been an educator for 25 years in Monroe, Escambia, Montgomery, Selma City and Conecuh counties. He served as President of the Conecuh Education Association, was a member of City of Evergreen Industrial Development Board and served 8 years as President of Evergreen District Congress of Christian Education. He is a certified foster parent. He has traveled abroad as a part of the 1996 Monroe County "To Kill a Mockingbird" Cast in Israel. Currently, he serves as Pastor of the West Side Missionary Baptist Church where he has pastored 20 years.

Manifest

APOSTLE KEITH L. MOORE

For the earnest expectation of the creature waiteth for the manifestation of the sons of God. (Romans 8:19 KJV)

About every 365 days, the world celebrates a new year in various venues. Revilers toast, dance, and spend a pivotal moment with people they loved and strangers who remained nameless. We entered into 2020 a few months ago with tinsel, balls droppings, giant apples falling from great towers as the church, Kingdom people, believers and the like offered praises to God for "making it over" and "shouts of victory" for what we anticipate in Christ. All of creation entered a new second, a new minute, new hour, a new day, a new week, a new month and a new decade in different time zones around the globe. How often do we do that? Well, the truth of the matter; is once every 10 years. Once every 10 years we experience a new second, a new minute, a new hour, a new day, a new week, a new month, a new year, and a new decade. That is eight new beginnings in the same space. In all of this, the world is left *groaning*, but the Kingdom is *manifesting!*

Manifestation, *Apokalupsis*, means to lay wide open so that something is seen or revealed. Manifestation is a disclosure of truth. God is revealing *the better you*. Let this resonate in your spirit. *God is revealing the better me. God is revealing the elevated me. God is revealing the tried me. He's revealing the greater me.* That marriage crisis, that family crisis, everything you've dealt with in crisis is going to produce Christ in you for the next season.

Believers are about to experience and amazing season in the Kingdom. It is about to be tremendous in your life. By faith, declare that this is my time of manifestation! It's going to be amazing even with all the crisis and frustrations of last year, even the last decade. Trust that you are bringing a fresh wisdom into your season of manifestation. You know how to handle some things now because you have wisdom from your last season.

We are about to enter effectual doors that are going to produce some amazing things in life born out of crisis. The truth of the matter is we were not tested for any random reason; we endured a season of proving for presentation. Both quality and character were being tested for the next level of presentation; the next level of functionality. The Father was maturing us. We learned, matured, grew in those seasons so that we are ready for the next level of presentation; the next level of manifestation. You're standing in a different place. You're going to stand in a different glory. "Arise and shine," Isaiah 60:1 KJV states, "thy light has come and the glory of the Lord has risen upon you." Why is the glory so difficult? Because a dark grossness has covered the earth. Out of the darkness comes more life.

Consider that your crisis has caused you to mature into the *answer* for someone's *problem*. Some equipment in life is built strictly for crisis. We are being used as we walk with Christ. You don't need ambulances when everything is calm. You don't need the police cruisers when all is well. A defibrillator is useless unless someone has a heart attack. Some equipment is built for the crisis. Your last season developed the *first responder* in you. We need some first responders in the kingdom. The world needs first responders. First responders are those folks who know how to go to a brother that's fallen with a spirit of meekness and humility that's overcome with a fault and help restore them. We're here for the crisis. Turn your lights on and get there for somebody else in this season.

Be there for somebody else in their crisis not like Job's friends with criticism, but like Christ with solutions. We need some first responders. I remember one of my former sons in the ministry and a brother to me now was going through EMT school. He had to learn many different things. He had to understand the human body. He had to understand what CPR was. He had to understand how to introduce an IV. He had to go through much training. He had to understand the intricate details and different functions of the body. He did all that training so that he could get to the field and perform a life-saving function in the moment of crisis. In like fashion, gifts, anointings, and callings are manifesting in the Kingdom to meet the crises of humanity.

Our training was essential, but trials are the proving grounds. Trials test suitability and performance. Trials measure the level of excellence. Don't cheat your way through the training. Who wants a doctor doctoring, who cheated their way through final exams and slept through the internship? Performance is affected by the quality of training.

Your suitability is going to be determined by the consistency of what you've learned. Do not pray to skip the lessons. Do not skip the training. Don't take the lazy man's way and be ignorant in the Word. Study to show yourself approved; a workman that needed not to be ashamed, rightly dividing the word of truth. Study your own unique gift, calling or anointing as you walk therein. Become a true practitioner of whatever gifts God has given you: MANIFEST!

Let's recall Esther from the Biblical story of her iconic rise from being an orphan to becoming a queen. Esther was chosen for such a time as this. She had a whole nation's destiny riding on her back. She and a whole nation was about to face a crisis. In the month of Tevet, she was put in Shushan to be tested, she had to be proven first. After preparation, there's proving. Esther was beautiful. Though she had favor on the outside, her character had to be tested on the inside. Esther was chosen for such a time as this.

When is your gift time? When does your perfecting meet God's purpose in someone else's circumstance? When does your perfection meet God's purpose in someone else's problem? Are you a first responder? Child of God, you have been built for *such a time as this*. So when is your "this"? When is your moment? Because you were in preparation last season, God was preparing you this whole decade of prophetic season 5770. The last decade was about you gaining wisdom. Now you are about to manifest. Like Esther, we have been tested to be ready for *such a time as this*.

Where is the excellence? Where's the quality? Where is the character? The product doesn't get to determine its purpose. The manufacturer determines the purpose and he puts the team in place to produce the proper product. Ephesians 4:11 teaches that Kingdom leaders are to prepare you for the work of the ministry, for the edifying of the body of Christ. Your quality has to be tested.

Are you loving like you are supposed to love? Are you sharing the love of Christ? Are you speaking the right things over the lives of other people? You must be tested and tried. Your performance must be measured. It must be proved.

I declare increase over your life. Whatever your given gift is, whatever your anointing is, it is about to manifest and produce, watch this, in warp speed! At higher rate. And you're not going to get tired doing it. You're going to rest in Christ. You're not going to give up. You're not going to give in. But the demand on your life is about to increase. Rest in that. Trust the Holy Spirit! Demand requires increased production.

The production is about to increase because of the demand. And I declare that the product that you are and the service that you render is going to be excellent! It's going to be excellent because you have been proven and tried. Like Job, when you come forth, it will be as pure gold.

The testing is to prove you have the strength of Christ rising up in you. Hallelujah, Jesus! Oh, God! Some of you, are going to form new connections. Every first responder needs a first responder. Every person who tends to crisis needs someone that can tend to them in their crisis. God said, there's no embarrassment in it, because every doctor needs a doctor.

Surgeons can't perform surgery on themselves. They need another surgeon to perform the surgery. You cannot anesthetize yourself and then start cutting. Hallelujah! You must be anesthetized, and then let somebody else be trusted with a scalpel. You must allow someone else practice their specialty on you. You cannot, watch this, you cannot administer the medicine and then be the healing too. You must let someone else doctor on you.

Paul on one missionary journey was lowered out the window to help him escape. There were times when the crowd had to had hide Jesus. And I'm telling you, the first responders need a first responder. Every pastor needs a pastor. Every leader needs to be led. Don't be an island unto yourself. Allow someone to cover your life! Allow someone to cover your life! You need it in this season if you're going to manifest all that God wants to manifest in your life.

Keith L. Moore is the Senior Pastor and Founder of iMpact Christian Church, and Presiding Primate Kingdom Agenda Fellowship, Montgomery, Alabama, which is in its seventh year of existence. He received his call and was licensed to minister in 1991. He was ordained in 1993 and has completed three pastorates to date at Water Oak Grove Baptist Church and Beersheba Christian Church, Prattville, Alabama, and Morning Star Baptist Church, Clanton,  Alabama. Apostle Moore also served with First Baptist Church, Greater Washington Park in Montgomery as an Associate Minister.

He has ministered as a Sunday School Teacher (Boys to Men Youth Group), Director of Drama and Bible Study Teacher. Consecrated Bishop in August of 2012 he went on to be affirmed as an Apostle in the Lord's Church on 12 October 2016/1 Tishri 5777. He has been a motivational speaker for years, speaking to local schools, colleges and universities, businesses, professional, social organizations and religious institutions across the state and regionally. He served the Morning Star Baptist Church for seven years.

Keith is a graduate of Troy State University at Montgomery with a Bachelor's in Psychology. He has begun work on his Master's degree in Biblical Studies at Faulkner University, Montgomery, Alabama. He served his country for 22 years as a member of the U.S. Air Force and United States Air Force Reserves. In addition to being a pastor-teacher, trainer, speaker, and author, Keith is the founder of Griot Poetry Society, and is an avid volunteer. He resides in Montgomery, Alabama with his wife Deleta M. Moore (Williams) of Birmingham. Keith is a father of six. He and Mrs. Moore have two children to their union, Kezia Lertrice and Zipporah Jamese.

Daddy's Little Girl: What I Tell My Daughter

JUDGE JR GAINES

"As a father shows compassion to his children, so the Lord shows compassion to those who fear him" (Psalms 103:13 ESV). Being a father is an honor. As a matter of fact, it might be the greatest honor with which God can bless us. Being a father is a direct reflection of God's identity as "Our Father" which Jesus uses in the model prayer. Some may not take this privilege seriously. Some may squander it carelessly. Some may be so afraid of the prospect that it paralyzes them. This final one is the sentiment with which I can most readily identify. But I am glad to say the fear of not knowing what to expect, what fatherhood would bring, and what it would cost me in every way did not stop me from entering into an agreement with my lovely wife to be not only her husband, but also the father to our children.

We have both a son and daughter. My son is 18, and my daughter is 14. I love them with my life. I, along with my wife, try to provide for all their needs and to make sure they have very few unfulfilled wants. As a father, I also show compassion to both of my children. Not just because the Bible requires compassion, but because my children - all children - deserve compassion. They are among the most vulnerable of humanity. They come into this world without asking to be born but depending on those who make them to take full, consistent, and thorough responsibility for their well-being and for making sure they experience uninterrupted compassion and love.

I never wanted to be a father who just screamed about all the wrong my children did. They would make mistakes, some more serious and disappointing than others, but I am grateful that I understood going in that they would not be perfect . . . I certainly wasn't growing up. So, I wanted to be a father who builds his children up. The way I accomplish this, however, is different for my son and my daughter. I think it is important to communicate with them differently – sharing the same principles, but in two totally different ways. My words of wisdom are usually the same, and my methods are uniquely designed to show them I would do anything for them.

My son gets a directive like "you better do this and do this now!" I am more direct because he is older: and he is a male. As a man, I know what my son will face as he becomes a man. Contrary to what he might believe at different times and based on my reactions to certain things, everything I do, every correction, every directive – EVERYTHING – is based on the fact that I love him, I want what's best for him, and know life will challenge him beyond belief as he matures as a Black man.

I know this is about my daughter, but I thought some background was required. My daughter usually gets less directive driven instructions and most often in a different tone. I speak to her, even in moments of correction, in a lighter tone because she is younger and because she is a female. Just as I know what types of things and challenges my son will face as a man, I have ABSOLUTELY NO IDEA what my daughter will face. This motivates me to want to protect her from all the unknowns of life. I want her to understand how she should be treated by males, and not raising their voice at her is primary.

My daughter is absolutely beautiful in her father's eyes. There is nothing missing, nothing lacking, nothing insufficient. She is the second perfect combination of her parents. But I want her to understand that her outward beauty is representative of all the other amazing things about her. I want her to know that she is to be respected at all times and by anyone with whom she has contact. I want her to understand that her intellect is the perfect companion to her dazzling appearance. As a father, I want my daughter to be keenly aware that along with my love for her, I have respect for the girl that she is, the woman she will become, and ALL the positive, life-changing contributions to society she will make during her lifetime. But I also have to tell her some things to watch out for as she travels the road of being a female, which again, I do not understand in the least.

I talk to my daughter about various topics like education, politics, religion . . . and boys. My wife's grandmother used to say, "Be particular." I didn't understand that phrase when I was younger, but now I do, and I tell my daughter just that: BE PARTICULAR. Being particular is more than just being careful. It also entails being selective about who you spend time with, where you go, and what you do. Without trying to put undue pressure and worry on her, I try to make abundantly clear to my daughter that sometimes she won't be able to control circumstances, but when she can, she should. This will mean thinking all the way through the consequences that could be attached to her actions. "Being particular" will enable my beautiful daughter to safeguard herself, her reputation, and her future from the traps and pitfalls that can accompany being a female (which, as a reminder, I do not understand in the least).

Since I am in the legal field, I understand the term "accomplice liability." In short, it means that a person *with a defendant* is just as guilty of breaking the law through bad acts as the defendant is (especially if they helped in any manner). I try to impress upon my children – my son and my daughter – to "be particular" and make sure they are selective about their friends, acquaintances, girlfriend, boyfriend, and ANYONE with whom they might be associated. I also tell them that being a Christian requires that we have Christian friends and mates. This can't be determined by what someone says, but through their actions in situations that might offer the opportunity to NOT act in a Christian manner.

Being a father makes me a better man. I want to be the example for both my children. I want both my children to see and know what a Godly father/husband looks like. And I often remind my daughter to settle for nothing less, and most of all, to "be particular" because this world is tough. It is filled with victories and defeats. I constantly talk to my daughter about the highs and lows and how to deal with each. I have instilled in both my children how important it is to have a relationship with God. That relationship will help with being particular. I will not always be here to protect her, but I can leave my beautiful daughter with some principles will keep her walking with the Father. And that is most valuable to me.

JR Gaines is a native of west Alabama and earned a bachelor's degree in Business Administration and a master's degree in Professional

Accountancy from Jackson State University. He went on to earn a law degree from the University of Alabama, and then a Master of Law in Taxation degree from Georgetown University in Washington, D.C. He has been active with several organizations including the Alabama State Bar Association, the American Bar Association and Troy Accounting Alumni.

Prior to his judicial election in 2014, Gaines was an attorney in private practice at Gaines Law Firm which was created to meet the needs of the community. The firm prided itself on offering large-firm results, while maintaining the small-firm atmosphere in its care for its clients. It was dedicated to representing individuals, families, corporations, and governmental entities by assisting them in resolving their problems or planning for the future. Admired for paying close attention to the details of his work, JR is a very outgoing person whose genuineness is the hallmark of all he does. His keen insight into legal issues makes him an asset to the Montgomery County judicial system.

After practicing law for more than thirteen years, JR is now serving as a Circuit Court Judge for Montgomery County, Alabama. JR's wife, Monet McCorvey Gaines, is currently a District Court Judge for Montgomery County. The two are the proud parents of Trey and Michaela Gaines.

Where the Heart Is: The Reason I Serve

Tosh T. Sevier, I

At a very young age, my heart longed to be a change agent in my community. I was an observant child who paid attention to the obvious angst that seemed to prevail in my community. Seeing the pain and dysfunction as I grew older, I started questioning everything. I wondered why everyone seemed so angry. My parents seemed to always be preoccupied or dreading the ensuing workday. Church seemed to be the opiate that most people looked to as a beacon of hope in what seemed to be ongoing nightmare. My heart longed for a magical remedy to all the suffering that seemed so commonplace.

Growing up in New England in the 1980s offered a kaleidoscope of perspectives. Massachusetts, long known for its liberal ideas, had inequalities that mirrored a socioeconomic imbalance that weighed heavy on the undereducated. Families simply couldn't make ends meet. In the face of these challenges many found it almost impossible to raise a healthy family. The stressful conditions set the stage for the systemic withering away of traditional family values. A myriad of structural disadvantages based heavily upon race and class created walls that seemed insurmountable. The trauma of economic anxiety at every turn forced many into a downward spiral of violence and drug abuse.

Many undereducated citizens found it extremely difficult to keep pace with a rapidly changing job market. The days of simple jobs that required little education had become a thing of the past. The industrial practices of old had taken a sharp turn towards technology. As globalization drove wages down, American companies turned to automation to increase productivity and minimize human error. Now that a machine could single handily accomplish the job of a few workers, many found themselves unemployed and under qualified.

In direct correlation to the scarcity of high paying jobs in the inner city, people were forced into low income communities overrun with drugs and desperation. Crime associated with the sale and use of illegal narcotics created a volatile atmosphere that many urban youth and elderly feared daily. Our communities were no longer a safe haven of nurturing support. Everyone seemed to be in a collective struggling to survive. Somehow a war zone had been created. Dealers and addicts saturated the community and the death toll began to rise. Killing rival dealers for territory became the rights of passage for aspiring drug lords leaving behind a trail of tears and broken homes.

Over time the doctors, lawyers, butchers, seamstresses, and other artisans left the community. The value of their businesses and the homes close by had fallen with the decline of the neighborhood. Businesses that once reflected the residents of that community were now closed and reopened by people with no personal connection to those communities. The diversity of capital also left, and the community was no longer attractive to new development. The financial ecosystem had been disrupted and the revenues no longer recirculated in that community.

Homeownership as a vehicle for wealth building was no longer real. The idea had slipped out of reach. Upward mobility was nonexistent. Renters were forced into predatory renting situations with new landlords who had no empathy for the lives they were disenfranchising. As homelessness increased, the overall appearance of these once thriving communities took a turn for the worse. I longed to understand what I could do to help transform the plight of my loved ones, while fusing together several concepts to help those the world calls helpless.

By the grace of God and Him seeing my heart, I was led to the answer I hadn't necessarily thought of before. The work model that could and would begin to cause substantive, life-impacting change was based in one word: **SERVICE**. Once I heard this clarion call in my spirit, my passion was ignited. It started by remembering my forgotten ones through weekly acts of kindness. To me, it didn't seem like anything monumental or earthshaking, but to those who were and are the recipients of these acts, it appears to make all the difference in the world.

Once I opened myself up to receive the answer to my perplexing question of *why,* God began to show me that why is not important: **HOW** is. How can I truly make a difference? Through **SERVICE** that would bring together likeminded people who had the same questions I did – and who wanted to see the answers manifest in a way that would bless the disenfranchised, the undereducated, the hurting, and the needy. Understand that when we seek a way to make a positive impact from a sincere heart, God will not only show us the way, but will provide us with the resources to get there.

For example, every Monday we deliver a load of fresh food to a local Housing Authority Complex through a partnership with our local Target Super Center. On Tuesdays we return to teach a Life 101 class that highlights topics such as entrepreneurship, leadership, emotional intelligence, social skills and urban agriculture. We provide pizza and other snacks to encourage attendance and participation. Our organization also feeds the homeless and working poor a hot meal every Wednesday evening. We have become a distribution hub for hygiene supplies and other essential items.

Once we began to **SERVE**, I could see our condition with new eyes. My people needed me and others who have found their way above their difficult circumstances to help them find the way. Somehow along the journey of success we tend forget those we left behind in the valley of hopelessness. Returning to assess the damage provided me a new perspective of so many unseen possibilities.

The youth we serve show me a picture of myself at that age. I am reminded of how I used to look up to the hustlers because of their power and resources. Having found a more suitable way to prosper, I realized I had managed to become the entrepreneur I hoped to be. It dawned on me that I could be a source of inspiration. I looked like the hustlers I idolized. Dedicating time to be active in at risk communities gives youth a new idea of success to consider. Much to my surprise the youth responded to my altruistic embodiment of "making it." Now I invest my time and resources in those at-risk communities from which I longed to escape. With the help of so many community partners, we help kids reach for their dreams.

SERVICE is a prayer that we activate by caring for someone in need. *Whose report will you believe?* I see our possibilities as endless and our future is bright! As the trees reach toward the sun, so shall our struggle lift us up where we belong – together. I didn't want to monopolize your time telling you all the things we do in our local Southwest community to gain your admiration. More importantly I wanted to journey through a reality that is far too common. It is my hope to inspire you to take your awesomeness back to the places where nobody gets to see the bright side. You are the greatness that someone needs to see to keep pushing. Just show up for someone who's expecting no one to care. Service to humanity is a debt we all owe. The future of our world is predicated on the love we choose to show today.

Tosh T. Sevier, B.S. President and Founder, Grooming Gods Albany, Georgia, Real Estate Developer, Serial Entrepreneur, and Philanthropist

Tosh Sevier is president and founder of Grooming Gods, a training center for aspiring stylists and for current stylists aiming to strengthen their skill set. He also operates his own salon, Living Legends, where he creates a space for men to not only be groomed, but to also build and strengthen one another.

Starting his career at the age of 13, Tosh has been grooming since that time. He moved into his first barbershop (Chop Shop) at 17 after being given the opportunity to do so by one of the pioneers in the Albany barbering community, Mr. Charles T. Price. He worked in three of the Price family's barbershops before opening his own shop. A man of social consciousness, Tosh opened his first business, Klippers That Care, a mobile barber shop catering to the needs of the mentally challenged and physically disabled. Understanding the need to become full owner of his own shop, he purchased the FaithWorks Salon and later, opened up Living Legends Salon. As the years have gone by, Mr. Sevier and his wife have built an impressive real estate portfolio consisting of several residential and commercial holdings.

An active member of the Albany and Southwest Georgia community, Tosh contributes to a number of social and community organizations. He is co-founder of Albany Fashion Week, an annual experience that brings fashion from around the globe to Albany, Georgia. He also spends time as motivational speaker, marketing consultant, entrepreneurial coach, philanthropist and has published a number of articles and commentaries.

Tosh is married to the lovely Tiffany (Mitchell) Sevier, a school principal and has two children, Jazzmine Mitchell and Tosh Jr. He holds the Bachelor of Science degree in Speech and Theatre from Albany State University and aspires to earn the Doctor of Jurisprudence.

Wendy R. Coleman is the 3rd daughter of Mr. & Mrs. Joseph & Ruby Coleman and shares this honor with her four sisters, Victoria, Mamie,

Shabra, and Monica. Her additional bright lights are 7 nieces & nephews and 8 great-nieces & nephews. Her numerous spiritual children make her the most joyful mother in the universe. They make her life rich.

A veteran higher education practitioner, Wendy has taught at Albany State University and at her alma mater, Alabama State University. She currently serves as Associate Professor and chair for the Department of Theatre & Dance there. Never satisfied with doing just one thing at a time, this Woman of God also owns Sweet, Sweet Spirit Publishing & JRC Event Center. She shares a vision for Coleman's Taste restaurant with her sister Shabra. They are trusting God for manifestation in due season.

Wendy accepted her calling into the ministry in 1996 and was blessed to witness and learn servant-ministry under Sr. Pastor & Co-Pastor Roosevelt & LaVerne Carter at First Monumental Faith Ministries in Albany, Georgia. She served as pastor of First Congregational Christian Church in Montgomery for 6 years. God's guiding led her to birth Reaching The Remnant Ministries in 2018 where God is showing abundant favor and miraculous advancement.

Other Published/Produced Works by W. R. Coleman

The Man of God: A Story about Forgiveness (Novel)
Born Again (Stage Play)
Let the Church Say . . . (Stage Play)

Woman of God: What is Your Report (Inspirational0

This is Our Story:
Learning, Loving, and Living Well with Diabetes
(Stage Play commissioned through the Bayer Dream Fund)

Printed in the United States
By Bookmasters